GW01366817

Glitter Girl

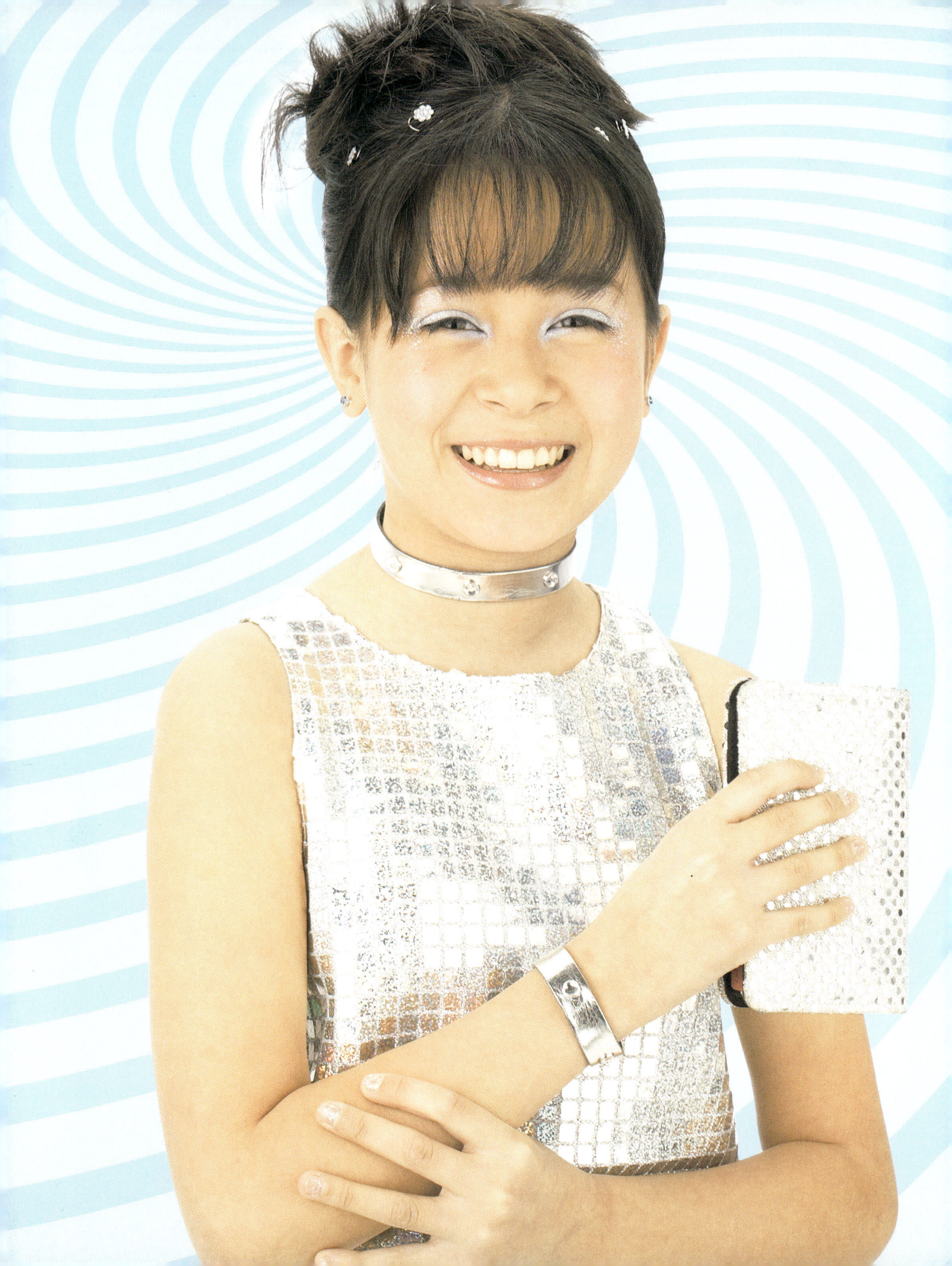

Glitter Girl

Christine Green

p

This is a Parragon book
This edition published in 2004

Parragon
Queen Street House
4 Queen Street
Bath
BA1 1HE, UK

Designed, produced and packaged by
Stonecastle Graphics Ltd

Edited by Gillian Haslam
Craft items made by Susie Johns
Photography by Roddie Paine

Copyright © Parragon 2001
All rights reserved. No part of this publication may be reproduced, stored in a retrieval system, or transmitted in any way or by any means, electronic, mechanical, photocopying, recording or otherwise, without prior permission of the copyright holder.

ISBN 1-40543-888-6

Printed in China

Contents

Going for Glitter	6		
Hair Accessories	8	Foot Perfect	36
Starry Styles	10	Jean Genie	38
Instant Impact	12	New Image	40
Glitter Face	14	21st Century Update	42
Stars in Your Eyes	16	Glitter Crazy	44
Luscious Lips	18	Vamp Re-Vamp	46
Funky Nails	20	The Right Trousers	48
Fancy Feet	22	Beautiful Belts	50
Jingle Jangle Jewellery	24	Glitter Tips	52
Razzle Dazzle	26	Take One Pair of Jeans...	54
Shining Examples	28	Sparkle at School	58
Fashion Fantasy	30	Fab Things to Make	60
Party Girl	32	Glitter Room	62
Glittermania	34	Fab Fingers	64

Going for Glitter

Want to be a disco-dancing diva and learn the tricks of how to look glitzy and glamorous? Then this is the book you've been waiting for.

It's packed with lots of fab ideas on how to add a sparkle to your make-up, create wild hairstyles using the latest accessories, make super sparkling jewellery, customize those summer T-shirts and even give your bedroom a new look.

Don't be a dull dude – go glitter and be the Queen of the Glitter Scene.

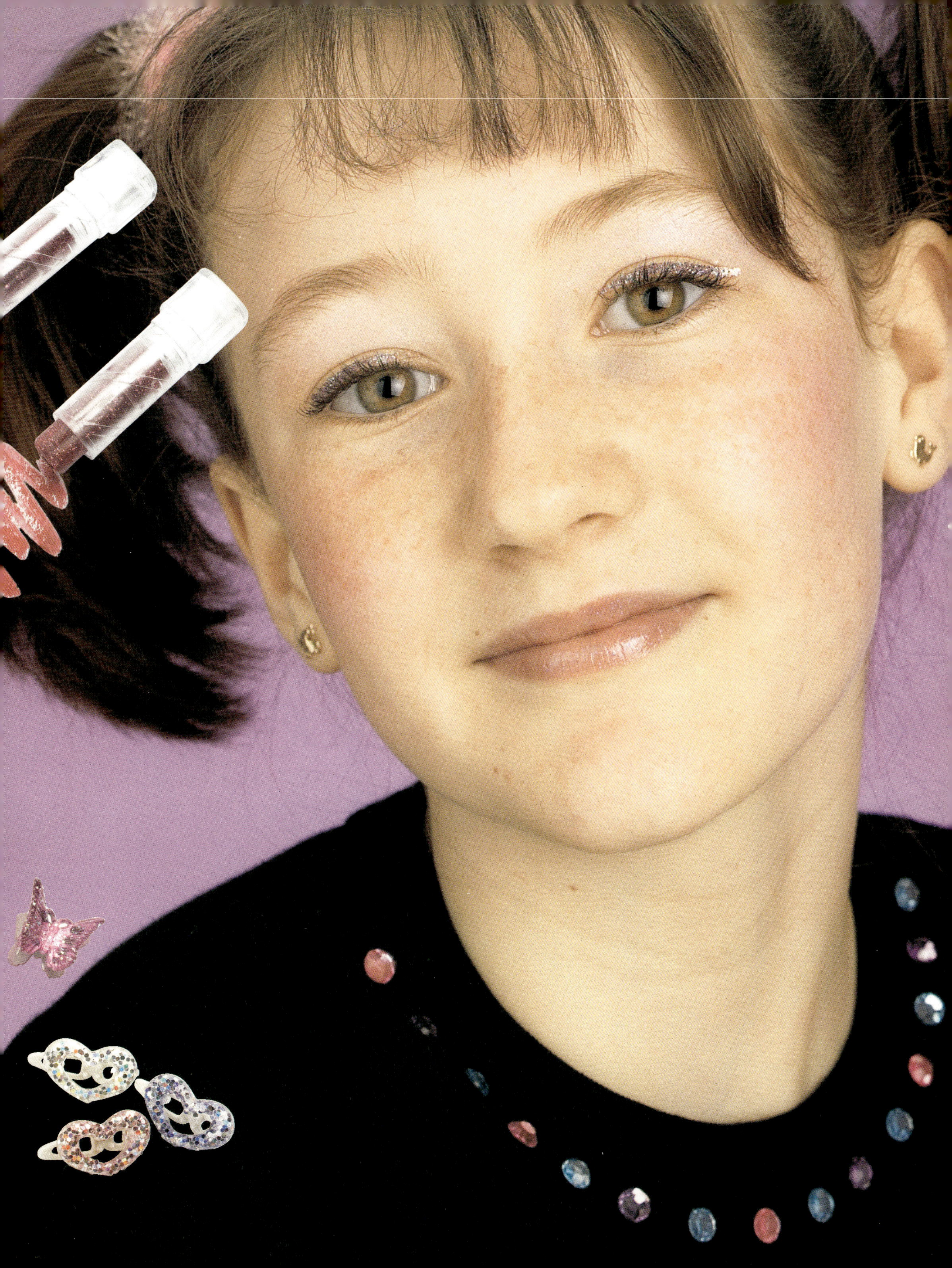

Hair Accessories

Fun and funky - this is what hair fashion is all about.

Slipping and Sliding

Clip back long hair with a couple of large crocodile claws. Choose spotted, plain, glittery or pastel shades, and for shorter hair there are even some funky coloured mini ones. Add a touch of glamour with hair combs and if they don't glitter, add some of your own! Go technic with metallic clips or star clips or choose one of the many others – round and sparkling, long and glittery, heart-shaped or patterned with animal prints. Wear them to hold the hair in place or as a hair accessory and don't forget plenty of those essential Kirby grips.

Wearing Hair High

Stretchy, fun and no more split ends when you wear bobble bands. Available in a rainbow of colours, one, two or even three in a ponytail look chic and for the summer disco, check out those with flower attachments. Beaded, glistening with tinsel, velvet, plain, checked, covered with feathers or, for a dramatic look, covered with false hair – scrunchies are a girl's number one hair accessory.

Wearing Hair Low

Hair bands look cool on long and short hair. Choose from shark-toothed silver bands, beaded, sequinned, plain or glittery, but if you really want to sparkle buy a tiara. Jazz up your tresses with haircoils, hairsprings, beads or haircuffs – all are great alternatives to hair slides. Turn heads with plaited or straight hair extensions, or clip on some coloured hair strands and try weaving ribbon into your plaits.

Hair Accessories 9

Looking for something different? Wow your friends with a cone-shaped Madonna-style ponytail holder, go Oriental with a couple of chopsticks or amaze everyone with a perfect bun spritzed up with some hair glitter.

Starry Styles

Bored with your hair down? Wear it up. Sick of it short? Buy a hair attachment. Looking for some fun hairstyles to try out, read on...

Chic and Classic

All the top stylists are using doughnuts when it comes to creating a perfect bun and it's so very simple. ☆ Sweep the hair up into a high ponytail. ☆ Slip the doughnut through the hair. ☆ Arrange the hair around the doughnut. ☆ Use Kirby grips to pin the ends underneath, or for that ruffled spiky look, spread the hair around the doughnut. ☆ Backcomb the ends slightly and complete the look with a spritz of glitter hairspray.

Bold and Haircuffed

Haircuffs are really easy to use, great for the party scene and perfect for thick or plaited hair. ☆ Plait a few thin sections of hair. ☆ Slip two or three haircuffs around thin plaits to add some sparkle. ☆ For a wacky look, get together with your mate and plait each other's hair all over, then slip haircuffs in and for an extra special shine, spray with glitter. One thing is for sure, you won't go unnoticed.

Starry Styles 11

Instant Impact

Have fun with temporary colours! Just the thing for that special occasion and simply washed out the next day. What could be easier?

Choose some of the many gels or sprays for instant colour. Always follow the instructions on the packet carefully.

Instant Colour

Fancy red hair, or how about blue, green, silver, gold or purple? Take your pick and choose from the range of fabulous false hair pieces available in wild or realistic colours. Or add streaks using hair lipsticks or hair mascara and if you don't like it, you can easily wash it out!

Glisten and Sparkle

Go girl go and make sure you sparkle under the disco lights with hair glitter. Spray it, roll it, draw it, paint it or gel it on – but most important of all, have fun wearing it.

Disco Diva Rave

This is a super hairstyle that can be easily adapted to suit any length of hair.
☆ Separate the hair into loads of small sections – it doesn't really matter how many. ☆ Take each section and pull it to the top of your head, twist until it forms a knot then hold down firm with some Kirby grips, leaving the ends to fan out. ☆ Spritz it with a firm hairspray, then add some onto your fingers and rub it into the spiky ends to make sure they really stand out. ☆ And for the final touch, slip some haircoils or even glittery slides around the rest of the hair.

Instant Impact 13

Glitter Face

If you want your skin to glow and look healthy, you're never too young to start taking care of it.

Face Care

Treat the skin to a monthly face mask and leave it feeling smooth, clean and tingling fresh. Masks are available in small sachets and tubes, ideal for all skin types. Invite some mates over and you can all try a different one – cucumber, sunflower, lime and coriander, tea tree – just rinse your face, slap it on and leave it to work.

Shimmer and Glitz

Feeling a little pale? Add a touch of colour with some blusher dabbed over the fattest part of the cheeks, then blend gently in. Shine with shimmer or for some true party sparkle, glisten with glitter.

Sparkle Like a Gem

Dazzle like a star with body gems and wear your heart on your cheek. Glow with stars or diamonds in silver, gold, blue, green or shimmering pastel shades. Wear them on the forehead, the cheeks, to the side of the eyes, on the eyebrows, or as nose studs. They even look sensational worn on the ears. Compact enough in pots or slim packets to slide in your purse for those occasions when your mate needs some sparkle in her life too.

Jazzy Gems

Body gems are easy to apply with a dab of Vaseline. Carefully lift them up using a pair of tweezers, dab a touch of Vaseline over the skin, pop the gem on the top, hold it in place for at least 30 seconds – and hey presto – the glittering princess!

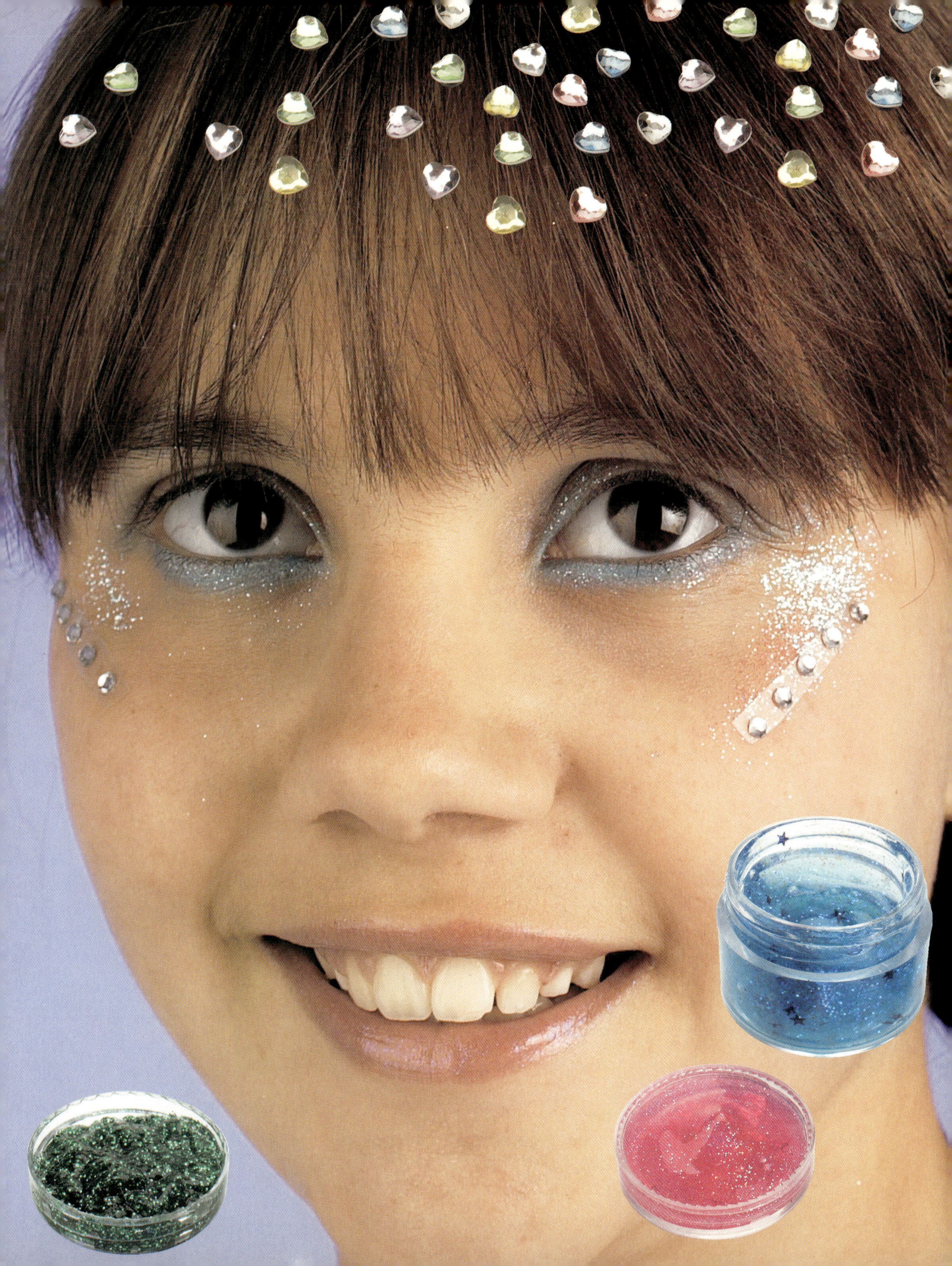

Stars in Your Eyes

Diamonds have always been a girl's best friend and so too are the range of sparkling eyeshadows.

Eye Spy

Available in pots, palettes, as creams, gels or even chunky crayons from shimmering gold to sparkling silver, from metallic blue to the softest shades of pinks, there are so many different types of eyeshadows and glitter crayons. If you still can't decide there are some amazing 'stick-on' eyeshadows you can buy which look just great.

☆ REMEMBER – some glitters might not be suitable for use around eye areas so always check the packet carefully.

Go for Gold

1 Slick gold eyeshadow over the eyelids and, using a brush, gently sweep some pink shadow up to the eyebrow. Blend it in.

2 Dab some glitter over the eyelids, use a couple of self-adhesive glitter eyeshadows or if you prefer, stick a couple of body gems at the side of the eyes.

3 Brush on one coat of black mascara. Leave to dry and then give those gorgeous eyelashes another coat.

Stars in Your Eyes 17

Don't forget the lipgloss. Finally, dust some glitter over the side of the cheeks. Well, doesn't every girl like to shine out at parties?

Luscious Lips

The only way to treat lips is to smother them with loads of lipgloss.

Lotta Lippy

There are some great colours available in pots, sleek tubes, palettes, stackers or mini lippies, ideal to slip inside your pocket or purse. Be passionate with pink, glitter with gold, stunning with silver, metallic blue, yellow, orange, red and bronze or pucker up those lips with some of the zany fruity lip pencils that not only look good but taste pretty great too.

Power to Lips

Smooth and soften lips with lashings of lipbalm available in sticks, lipstacks, and pots. Choose from mint, crazy kiwi, cherry, strawberry, lip smacker bubblegum, tropical passion or how about chocolate – yummy! They're also great for keeping lips soft in winter when the cold and wind can chap them.

Pretty Lips

Pretty lips are always noticed. Wear some lip liner, to define the lips – it also helps to keep lippy in place.

☆ Choose a liner that closely matches your lipstick shade. ☆ Carefully draw around the outline of the lips. ☆ Make sure the lips are fully covered by using a lipbrush – or you could always use a cotton bud.

☆ Dab the brush gently on to the lipstick and carefully fill in the outline you have already drawn.

☆ Press a tissue against the lips (this helps the lipstick remain on longer), then finally apply another coat.

Luscious Lips 19

Gloss and Go
Luscious lips have got to have lipgloss, available in tubs, squeezy tubes, tubes with applicators and rollerballs. There are some super colours from which to choose: red, gold, silver, plum, peach, bronze, glitter colours or play safe and wear clear lipgloss - you can always dab some loose glitter over the top.

Funky Nails

To show off your glittering nail polish, don't forget to pamper your hands and smooth on loads of handcream, massaging it deep into the skin and around the nails.

Glittery Nails

Cover the nails in loads of glitter nail polish, such as silver, gold, bronze or dynamic blue, or wear a plain colour and before it dries sprinkle with glitter.

Say It in Pictures

Can't be bothered painting the nails? Leave them clear and decorate with cool nail art stickers, create your own designs with nail pens, stun your mates with

Nails in a Second

Trying to grow your nails and not having much luck? You can always buy some false nails and when your friends see them, they'll never believe they aren't real!
☆ It's important that the nails are clean before you begin, so if you've any nail polish on, take it off and wash your hands. ☆ Do not use if you have cut or infected skin near the nails.
☆ Sort out the nails in the pack that best fit your own – you can always file them if necessary. ☆ Using a pair of tweezers, lift up a sticky tab that fits your own size nail and gently peel it away from the backing. ☆ Lay it down on your nail and then remove the protective backing before applying the false nail on top. Then press firmly. ☆ Now you can have fun painting and decorating your new nails and no one will ever believe they aren't real. ☆ To remove, simply peel off carefully.

Funky Nails 21

glistening hologram transfers, glisten with nail gems, add glittery tattoos or give them a totally Oriental make-over by painting the nails in black or white nail polish and then decorating with some Japanese transfers.

Hologram Designs

Spice up nails with hologram designs. If applied properly they won't rub off, even when temperatures are rising.

Two-tone Nails

Paint fingernails with a zany bright colour – two coats should be enough. When dry, paint the tips only in a glittery nail polish. You might need to apply several coats depending on the colours you choose: purple nails and silver tips, black nails and silver tips, white nails and red tips, or go totally overboard and paint each nail a different colour.

Fancy Feet

Feet were made for dancing, but before getting into action, give them some pampering.

Go Boogie

To keep those feet soft and smooth, massage foot lotion in after having a bath, walk around the house barefoot and give them a special treat – a cream foot talc to make sure they remain dry and fresh whilst you spend the night dancing. There are some lovely scents to choose from, such as balm mint or how about ice blueberry? Just sprinkle it on and feel those feet spring into action!

Paint Those Toes

Polished toenails look fantastic, especially when wearing open-toed sandals. Give them a couple of coats of nail polish, such as ravishing red or pretty pink pastel and to make sure you don't get too many smudges, nestle the toes into a funky toe divider or stuff pieces of cotton wool in between each toe when painting.

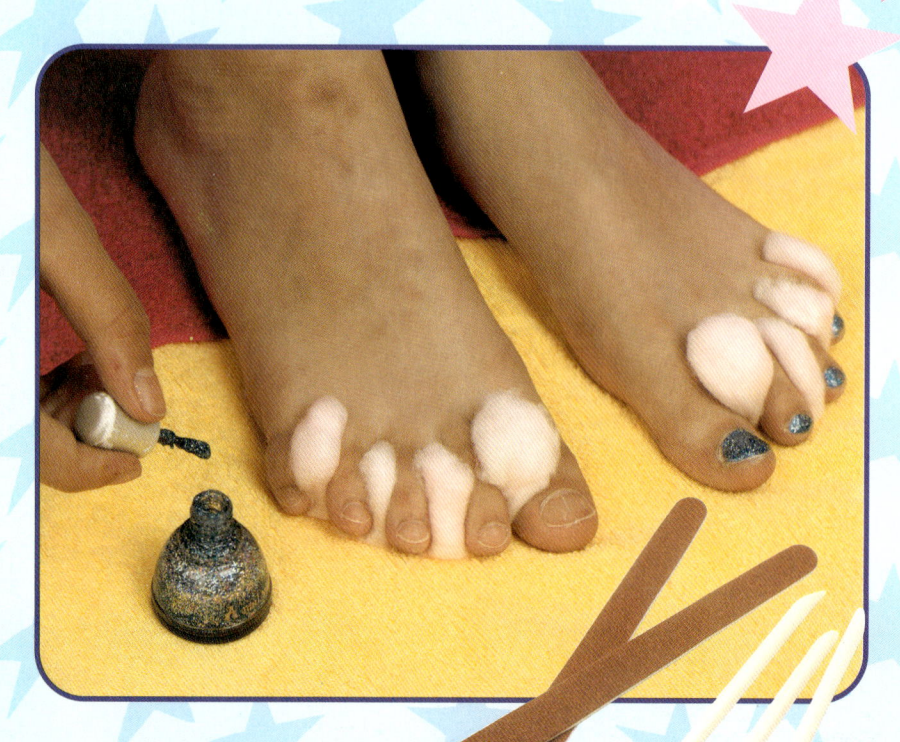

Pretty Toes

Why should the feet miss out on all the glamour? If you don't want to polish the toenails add some nail tattoos instead, or there are some super toe rings that slide on – just what's needed to flaunt off those new sandals.

Fancy Feet 23

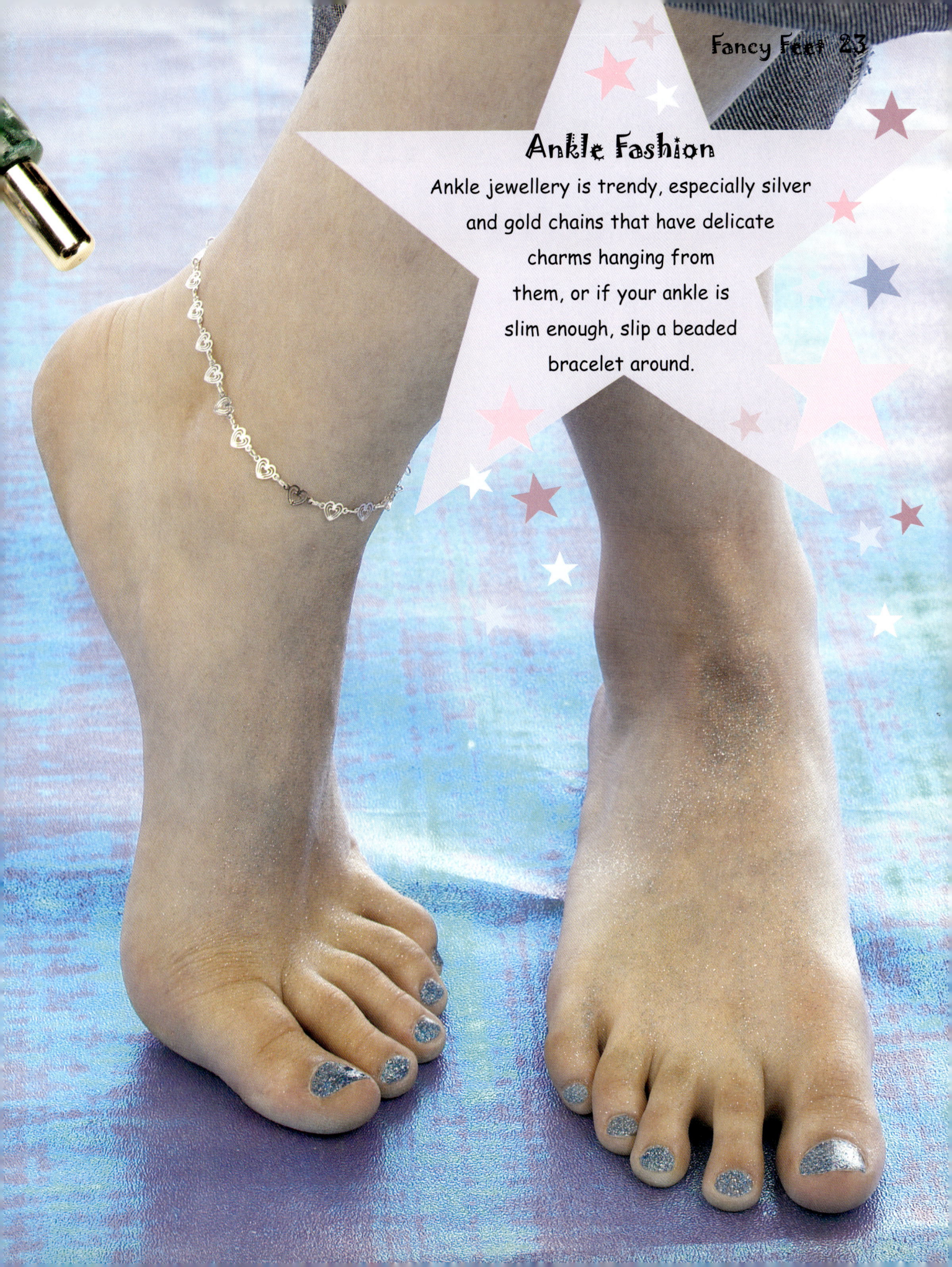

Ankle Fashion

Ankle jewellery is trendy, especially silver and gold chains that have delicate charms hanging from them, or if your ankle is slim enough, slip a beaded bracelet around.

Jingle Jangle Jewellery

Go for gold or swing for silver – it doesn't matter which but wearing bracelets and necklaces is a must!

Bangles and Chains

Jingle jangle on the disco floor with silver, gold or coloured bracelets, the more the merrier. ☆ Crystal or beaded, it doesn't matter as they all look cool. With peace beads and karma bracelets, different colours have different meanings. ☆ Look chic and elegant with a slinky chain bracelet or wear an armband on the upper part of the arm in silver, gold or pretty crystal beads. ☆ Be fashionable and wear a couple of plain silver or gold chains – perhaps one with your name or initial attached, dazzle everyone with a trendy tassel necklace, or a feminine chain with a silver encrusted cross. ☆ Chokers are cool and a number one jewellery accessory. ☆ Thin wires that fit snugly around the neck with a pretty droplet or feather attached are also popular.

Under a Wrist

Keep it under your collar, but cuffs are the trendiest item of jewellery; beaded, sequinned, leather, denim – they're all great fun, wear one or more together!

Jingle Jangle Jewellery 25

Razzle Dazzle

It doesn't matter how many pairs of earrings a girl has, it is never enough.

Large and Loopy

Huge loop earrings in gold or silver are hip for the disco scene, but if you don't like large loops there are also smaller ones available and, for a bit of fun, there are even some with attachments. You could always add some of your own, such as a Polo mint for when you're feeling peckish or a couple of large crystal beads. And if you want your earrings to match your outfit, brighten them up with a quick coat of nail polish.

Studs

Sparkle and glisten with studs in gold, silver, crystal or if you're feeling romantic, buy some heart or star-shaped ones. Small pearl studs look elegant or go all out for the 'star look' with a pair of drop diamanté earrings in slinky silver.

Better still, why not buy a packet with several different pairs and in that way if you get tired of wearing one set, you'll always have another to change to.

What Else?

No need to miss out on all the fun if you don't have your ears pierced – there's some trendy clip-on earrings in the shops, stick on a couple of glistening gems or wear an ear cuff on the upper part of the ear lobe.

☆ *For those with sensitive ears it's best to buy hypoallergenic earrings.*

Razzle Dazzle 27

Shining Examples

Get ready for some action and hit the streets to seek out the latest funky accessories.

Be Noticed

Have fun wearing a feather boa or snuggle up into a furry wrap, be trendy with a lacy shawl slung around the hips or on the shoulders, or 'howdy partner' with your very own cowgirl hat – if it's plain add some glitter to make it shine.

Go under cover behind a pair of diamanté-studded sunglasses and use a glittering gold wand to turn everyone into a frog except the cute guy you fancy, and if you want to surprise him, don't forget to pick up a fun party mask.

This and That

Jewellery fans are going to love shopping for toe rings for the summer. Belly chains look classic around a bare stomach and hand jewellery with an attached ring is perfect for an unusual look.

On The Line

If you own a mobile phone, check out some wild and wicked cover designs including fake animal skins, crushed velvet with stuck on jewels, vivid pink or stylish silver, and even better – you can buy attachable jelly numbers that actually sit over the real ones.

Shining Examples 29

The Essential Bag

Every girl needs a bag – where else can she carry her lipgloss for the evening? This one is small, sequinned, sparkling and great for the evening.

Fashion Fantasy

For the fashion-conscious miss who's gotta look good.

Hair

A smart look for mid-length to long hair. ☆ Divide the front of your hair into two sections and make up two plaits which will be swept back into the ponytail. ☆ Carefully brush the hair, including the plaits, back into a low ponytail. ☆ You can leave the ponytail loose or continue to secure it into a more formal style as follows. ☆ Twist the ponytail around so it rests against the head and the ends are sticking up. Hold it in place with Kirby grips and spritz with some hairspray to keep it firm. ☆ Spike out the ends of the ponytail, then rub gel into them with your fingertips. ☆ And as a final touch, slip some hair beads in.

Face

For a truly dazzling effect, try this...

YOU WILL NEED: Gold eyeshadow • mascara • glitter • lipgloss
☆ Sweep gold eyeshadow over the eyes and gently work it up into the eyebrows. ☆ Use a cotton bud to dab a small amount underneath the eye. ☆ Dab some glitter on the eyelids and up to the crease in the eye socket area. ☆ Flatter those eyelashes with a couple of coats of mascara. Make sure one coat is dry before applying the next. ☆ Stick a couple of gems or glitter by the side of the eyes. ☆ And to complete the look, slap on the lipgloss.

Fashion Fantasy 31

Party Girl

It's party time and that means one thing – dressing up and having lots and lots of fun.

Disco Diva Sparkle

Make sure you sparkle at the disco.

The Hair

A special occasion calls for a special hairstyle – a chignon, what else? And it's easy to do if you follow these simple instructions. ☆ Brush the hair to one side. ☆ Beginning at the bottom of the neck and working up to the top of your head, slip a row of Kirby grips along the middle of the back of your head to secure the hair to one side. ☆ Brush the hair back into a low ponytail then lift it up and twist it back in the direction of the Kirby grips until a roll is created. ☆ Leave the top ends free to fall loose. ☆ Push more Kirby grips into the edge of the roll to make sure it holds firm and then change the direction of some so that they go under the roll. ☆ When finished, jazz it up with hair beads, or give it a sparkle with some silver spray. ☆ *Don't worry – it might sound a bit complicated but if you follow each of the steps carefully you'll be amazed with the results. Have a trial run with some friends first.*

Party Girl 33

The Rest
☆ Rub some Vaseline over the eyelids and cover with glitter; dab some shimmer on the eyebrows. ☆ Be the jewel in the disco and stick a bindi on your forehead. ☆ Apply loads of plain lipgloss over the lips and dab glitter over for that extra sparkle.

Glittermania

Bored with your old clothes and fashion accessories but can't afford anything new? Don't worry – here are some fab ways to update what you have and make all your friends believe it's new.

Jazz Up Your Jewellery

☆ Measure strips of velvet to the size of your neck (with some overlapping) and then decorate with sequins or beads. Stick some Velcro on to fasten around the neck. ☆ Buy a plain leather or denim choker band and customize with small metal studs – do the same with a matching wrist cuff. ☆ Paint old bangles with glittery paint or wrap tinsel or fur fabric around them to give them a truly original look.

Hair Care

If you've some old hair scrunchies, don't throw them out. Why not...
☆ Cover them with tinsel. ☆ Sew sequins or beads all over. ☆ Decorate with glitter pens. ☆ Brighten up plain hair clips or Kirby grips with plain or glitter nail polish – use two or more colours for a dazzling effect. ☆ If you don't have glitter polish, use an ordinary polish and before it dries, sprinkle craft glitter over the top. Finish off with some clear nail polish to hold the glitter firm.

Customize Your Clothes

☆ Add sequins or braid to T-shirts, cardigans and jumpers to bring them right up to date. ☆ Jazz up an old jacket or revitalize an outgrown pair of jeans with gems, motifs, sequins, buttons and patches. ☆ Make cool accessories for your room and as super gifts for your friends and family.

Glittermania 35

You'll be amazed how creative you can be! The following projects show you how...

Foot Perfect

Give an old pair of trainers a new lease of life.

Customized Trainers

Make sure the trainers are clean and if not, pop them into the washing machine but you'd better ask an adult first. Customize them by painting with silver stripes or use glitter pens/paint to create your own unique design. Here's how we made ours:

YOU WILL NEED:
Newspaper • fabric glue • coarse silver glitter • silver fabric paint • diamantés • silver pompoms

☆ Remove the laces.
☆ Make sure you've put loads of newspaper down to protect the table or floor (it might even be best to do this outside).
☆ Spread fabric glue over sections of the trainers, sprinkle with coarse silver glitter and leave to dry.
☆ Shake off the excess glitter over the newspaper and save for another project.
☆ With silver glitter fabric paint, draw swirls and lines along the stitching.
☆ Glue a row of fake diamonds (diamantés) along the front of each trainer.
☆ Replace the laces with ribbons and glue or stick silver pompoms to the ends.

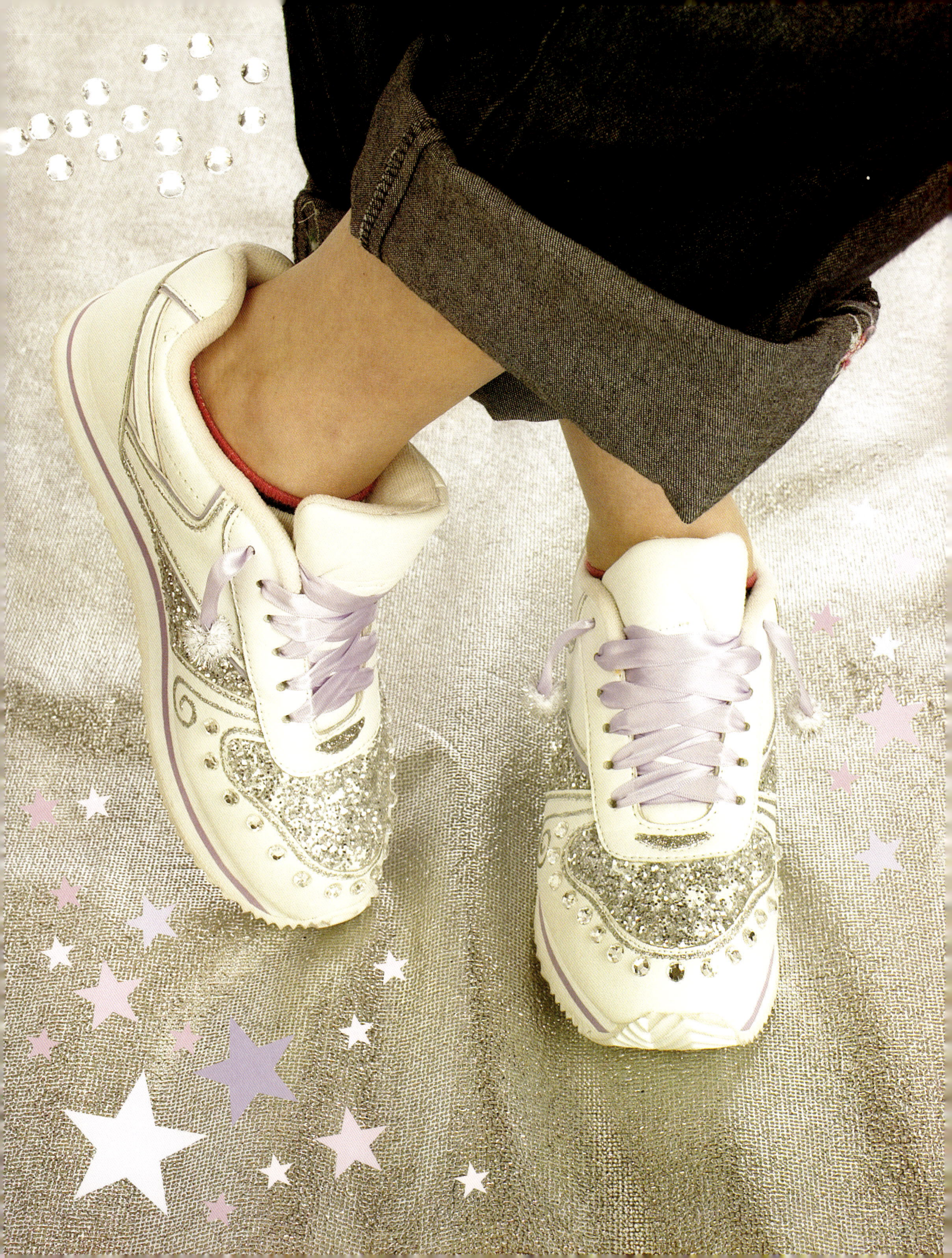

Jean Genie

Everyone owns at least one pair of jeans, but if yours are beginning to look a little dated and could do with some cheering up, why not modernize them?

Go For Braided

This is a great way to create a stunning new look, but you could also make up your own designs.

YOU WILL NEED: Braid • ric rac • sequins • gems • shisha mirrors (take a look around your local haberdashery store and you'll find loads of different designs) • needle and thread • tape measure • scissors

☆ Remove the waistband from the jeans and fray the raw edge. ☆ Cut off the hems from each leg and fray. ☆ Add rows of braid and ric rac – it's always a good idea before gluing or sewing anything in place to make a rough design where you want to stick everything before you begin. ☆ Measure along the bottom of the jeans and then cut lengths of braid and ric rac to fit. ☆ Pin the braid onto the jeans. Then tack to keep it firm for sewing later. ☆ After finishing one leg, do the other one but make sure they match. ☆ Then using small stitches with a matching coloured thread, begin sewing the braid firmly on to the jeans.
☆ If your jeans have a small tear or a hole, instead of covering it up – make it bigger! Cut out a square hole and fray the edges. Then put some fabric underneath and stitch in place. ☆ Stick or stitch on circles of fabric and edge each circle with glittery fabric paint. ☆ Sew on little flowers cut from a length of daisy braid. ☆ Glue tiny gems over the top part of the jeans for the finishing touch.

Wash by hand and remember to turn them inside-out first.

Jean Genie 39

New Image

Add your own personal touch to cardigans and jumpers.

Bold and Beautiful

An easy make-over to transform a plain cardigan into something truly original!

YOU WILL NEED: Plain cardigan • lace • pins • tape measure • matching coloured thread • needle • pearl beads • iron-on patch • glitter fabric paint • fancy buttons

☆ Measure and cut out two lengths of lace long enough to fit down both sides of the buttonhole bands and around the neck. ☆ Pin and tack it in place. ☆ Using thread the same colour as the braiding, stitch coloured lace up the front of the cardigan, beside the buttonhole band, around the neck and down the other side of the front. ☆ Stitch pearl beads to each point of the lace. ☆ Apply an iron-on flower patch, adding a touch of glitter fabric paint. ☆ Replace the buttons with flower-shaped ones.

More Ideas To Jazz Up That Cardigan

☆ Lace always looks pretty, especially if edged along the neckline. ☆ Sew different coloured or sized beads over the front, design a fake pocket out of sequins or buy a motif and sew it on, adding diamantés for that extra sparkle. ☆ Who wants reminding of their old school jumper? Cover it with embroidered motifs and, to make them slightly different, sew using different coloured threads. ☆ Use some colourful glitter pens and give it your own look!

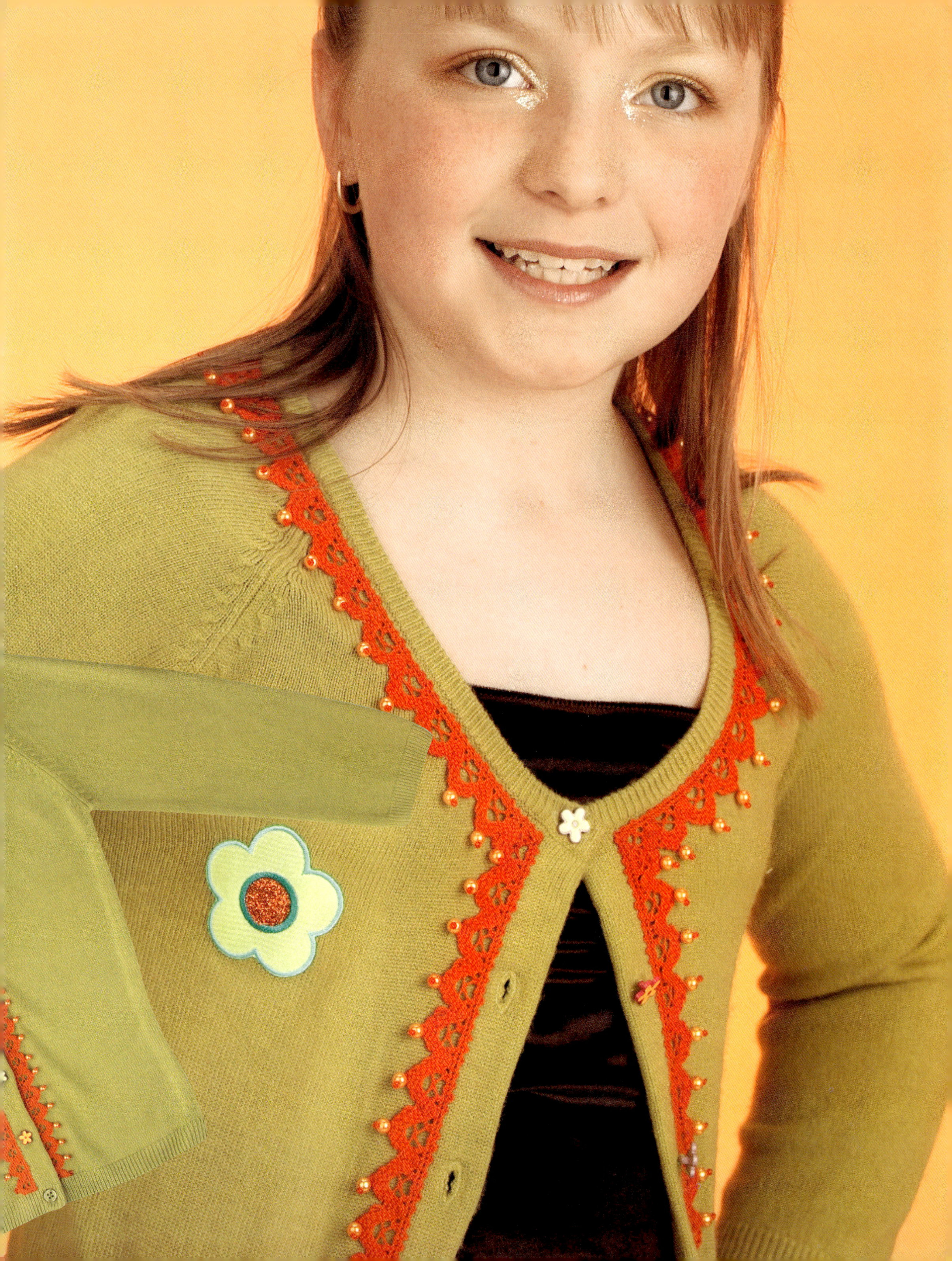

21st Century Update

An old denim jacket is no use sitting in the wardrobe. It will do far more good if you get it out and jazz it up.

Dazzling Rainbow

A special girl needs a special jacket and this is such a stylish design, you could wear it at a party.

YOU WILL NEED: *Lengths of sequin trim in rainbow colours • pins • thread to match • needle • scissors • sequins*

☆ Lay your jacket on the table. ☆ Cut lengths of sequin trim in different colours to fit across the front of the yoke on each side and pin in position. ☆ Do the same around the collar and pocket flaps. ☆ Stitch in place. ☆ Stitch on individual sequins, too, and surround some of them with circles of sequin strips.

Update Ideas

There are loads of way to glam up a denim jacket and if you are good with a needle and thread you can have great fun changing the way it looks. ☆ Buy thin lengths of leather or suede in varying sizes and sew them at intervals up the sides of either arm. Great worn with your cowgirl hat! ☆ Buy studs – the type that rock 'n rollers wear on their leather jackets – and glue them on the back in a groovy design. ☆ Dazzle mates with a dynamic denim jacket by edging the collar and around each of the cuffs with diamantés.

Creating your own design is all about making a fashion statement and if you're short on ideas, flick through magazines or take a look in the top high street stores.

Glitter Crazy

Get out last year's T-shirts and customize them to your own special design.

Bold and Bright

YOU WILL NEED: Cardboard • pen and paper • scissors • sticky tape • T-shirt • fabric glue • gems • fabric paint • paintbrush

☆ You will need a stencil. To make this, trace whatever shapes or letters you intend using on to a piece of cardboard and cut them out. ☆ Decide where you intend placing them on your T-shirt and hold in position with sticky tape.

☆ Carefully outline the design in pen, fill in the shapes with fabric glue and then sprinkle with glitter. ☆ Or you could trace around the stencils with a glitter pen. Or trace around the stencil and decorate with gems or beads. ☆ If you are painting the design, dip your brush into some paint and dab it over the top of the stencil (you could also use a small sponge), and to make the colour brighter go over it again. ☆ Once dry peel away the stencil – how easy is that?

☆ It might be a good idea to do this project outside on a calm day during the summer.

Starry Styles

☆ Show everyone what a groovy chick you are and cut out large stars from some glittery fabric. Then glue them over your T-shirt. ☆ Buy unusual beads or sequins and sew them around the neckline of a plain T-shirt to look as if you are wearing a necklace. ☆ Fake gems can be glued on using fabric glue.

Sew a glittery motif on to a plain T-shirt and edge the neck with a colourful braid.

46 Glitter Girl

Vamp Re-Vamp

Look in your fave magazine and check out the top high street stores for the latest look in T-shirts to see if you can re-vamp some of yours.

Versatile Vests

Don't forget those summer vests that only appear once or twice a year.

Glitter Glamour Girl

Look out for fabulous sequin motifs at your haberdashery store. They come in brilliant colours and are so easy to use – simply sew, stick or iron on!

Go For Glitter

Use a gold glitter pen and draw circles over the T-shirt or if you're feeling creative, design stars and moon shapes out of glittery fabric and glue them on.

Cover-up

Cover the straps with sequins or cut out some glittery fabric and stitch it over the front.

Boob Tube

If you have got time and you have an old boob tube that needs re-vamping, why not buy loads of sequins and set to work carefully sewing or perhaps better still, gluing them all over.

Sparkle with Gems

Better still, why not glue small gems diagonally across the vest, making the perfect top to wear for that summer barbecue!

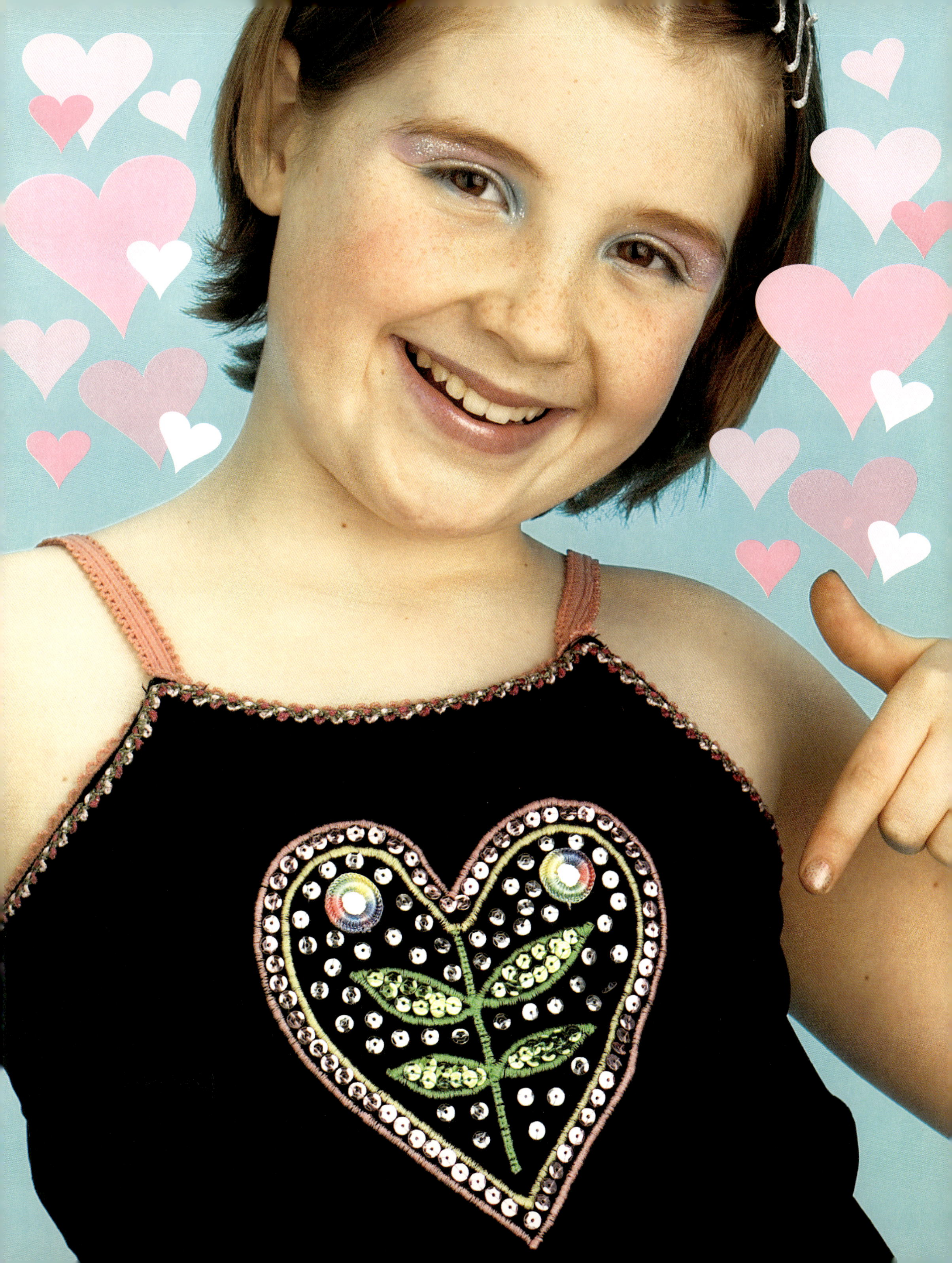

48 Glitter Girl

The Right Trousers

Plain trousers in desperate need of modernizing? Why not dig them out and use all that money saved by revamping them to buy some glittery make-up?

Cool for Summer

These cool khaki summer trousers look sensational with a touch of glamour. Jazz them up using gold sequin stars and studs. Push gold-coloured metal studs through the fabric and bend the points inwards on the wrong side to keep them in place. Thread a gold chain through the belt loops and sew sequin stars to each end.

Classic and Stylish

If you've an old pair of navy blue or black trousers give them a totally new look. Make up a design on some paper, draw around it onto a piece of cardboard and then cut it out. You've now got a fab stencil to transfer wherever you like on your trousers using glitter pens or even diamantés to go around it.

Less is More

If your trousers have shrunk slightly or you have grown too tall for them, don't throw them out. Just simply trim them higher up so they are at mid-calf length, turn over the hem and cover the bottom edge with some pretty braiding.

Hippie Hipsters

If you don't want to add anything on to your trousers, why not take something away, such as the waistband to give them a hipster look. Then wear with a slim chain belt slung around your hips.

The Right Trousers 49

Beautiful Belts

Belts are here to stay and it doesn't matter what size you are, they can look super worn with trousers, a skirt, a dress or even looped around a bare stomach.

If you haven't got any belts, ask mum or dad or an older sister for their old ones (you can make them smaller by adding extra buckle holes) and you can have a great time making them glitter.

Go Glitter

Thin glittery belts can really add a sparkle to any outfit.

YOU WILL NEED:
Thin belt • craft glue and varnish (both available from art shops) • glitter • paintbrush • fake gems

Warning – put loads of newspaper down on the area where you are working – or better still, work outside on a calm day. ☆ Cover the belt with glue and then sprinkle glitter evenly along, making sure the belt is well covered. ☆ Leave it to dry. ☆ Carefully lift up the belt and then, in order to make sure the glitter remains, paint a coat of varnish over the top and glue fake gems on top.

☆ Result – one very trendy belt that would cost a lot of money to buy in the shops.

Pure Colour

Instead of using glitter, paint the belt and when dry, give it a coat of varnish to prevent the paint peeling off. Then personalize it with some trendy studs.

Chain Belt

A thin belt lying across the hips looks really chic but if you don't have one use paper clips. It's original and if they're gold or silver, who would know the difference?

Beautiful Belts 51

Glitter Tips

Glitter isn't just to wear for parties or discos – it can really add a sparkle and twinkle to daytime wear too.

Be Cool and Keep Warm

Keep hands keep warm and stylish by sewing sequins or beads around the cuff of gloves. ☆ Make a design on the front of each using beads or write a fun message using fabric paints and glitter or you could buy some motifs and sew these over the front. ☆ Or simply sew a band of fake fur around the cuffs and create a decorative motif on the back of each glove.

Sparkling Socks

Brighten up socks and cover them with cute glitter star shapes. Sew coloured beads, braiding or sequin trim around the top.

Heads is the Winner

Got a plain baseball cap? Transform it into a sparkling cap using glitter pens or puff paint, cover it with masses of sequins or sparkling studs. You'll have great fun doing this – make a rough design on paper before putting it on to the hat.

Glitter Tips 53

Take One Pair of Jeans...

Jeans too small? Don't throw them out as there are loads of simple things you can make out of one pair.

Shoulder Bag

Every girl needs a bag to carry her important bits and pieces in and denim bags can sometimes be quite expensive in the stores.

YOU WILL NEED: Old pair of denim jeans • needle and thread • scissors • tape measure • pen

☆ Turn the jeans inside out.
☆ Measure down from the waist to the crotch (this is the point where the legs of the jeans begin). ☆ Draw a level line across and cut the legs off. ☆ Using a double strand of thread sew the two ends together. ☆ Turn the jeans back on to the right side. ☆ The strap is next. ☆ Cut a length of material from what remains of the jeans, measuring approximately 60cm (24in) long and 10cm (4in) wide. ☆ Fold it in half so the inside of the material is showing.
☆ Sew up one end and down the length, then turn the material inside out so that the 'right' side is showing. ☆ Sew up the remaining end. ☆ Place the strap on opposite sides of the bag and sew firmly into position using double thread.
☆ Leave the bag as plain denim or jazz it up and add some beads or sequins.
☆ If you have a sewing machine in your house, it is a good idea to ask an adult to go over the stitches to strengthen the bag.

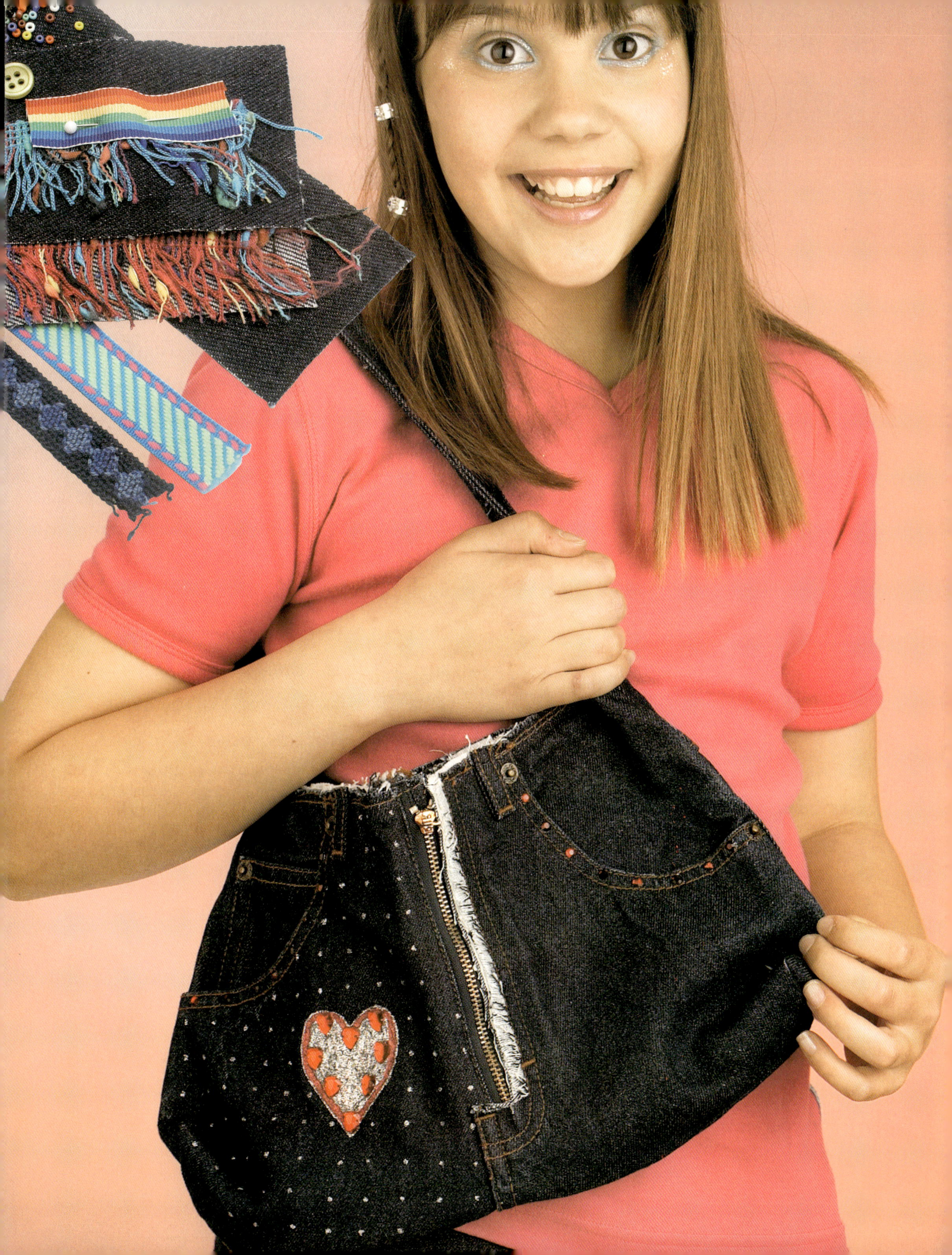

56 Glitter Girl

Notebook Holder

This is something else you could make from an old pair of jeans – stitch this zany little notebook holder to store all those secret messages.

YOU WILL NEED: Two back pockets • needle and thread • scissors • glue • sequins • press stud or Velcro • fabric glue • fringing, sequins or beads

☆ Remove both back pockets by cutting through the stitching. ☆ Stitch them together with right sides facing using double thread. ☆ Sew down one side, along the bottom and up the other side leaving the top open. ☆ Turn back over on to the right side and, halfway along the centre, stitch a press-stud or glue some Velcro on. ☆ Decorate with multicoloured bead fringes, sequins or beads or almost anything.

Belt Up

This will be the easiest and trendiest belt you have ever made. ☆ Remove the waistband from the jeans by cutting through the stitches. ☆ Before stitching the two sides together, insert some fringed braid. ☆ Decorate with beads or glitter paint. ☆ Or add studs, beads, sequins or use glitter pens to create your designs.

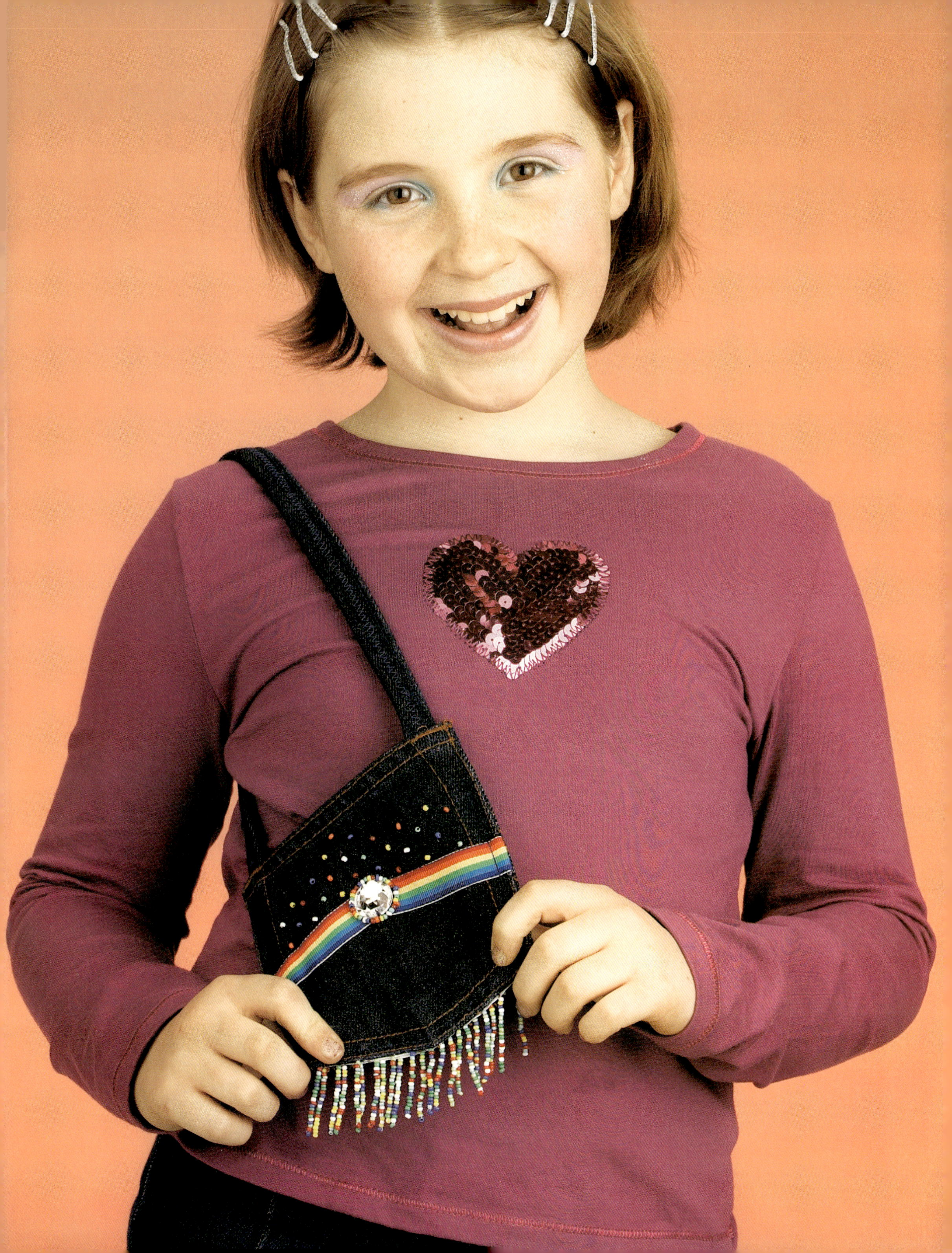

Sparkle at School

Girls just wanna have fun – and you can too, even when going to school.

School Files

Use glitter pens to jazz up a plain school file. ☆ Doodle a character, or edge it with sparkly sticky tape. ☆ Cut out some pictures of your fave bands, stick them on the file and circle with glitter. ☆ You could cover your file with some aluminium foil, but before doing so lay the sheet over a bumpy surface, such as the pavement or the rough side of corrugated cardboard, then gently flatten it by running over it with the side of a pencil. The pattern will appear, creating a very distinctive look.

Pencil Case

Revive your old pencil case. ☆ If it's plastic, cover it with stars made from foil. ☆ Cut out different shapes from coloured paper – or be a devil and cover it totally with double-sided sticky tape and stick on some fluffy fur fabric (you can buy scraps in different colours from fabric stores).

Glammed-up School Bag

Add some glitz and glam to a boring school bag. ☆ Use glitter pens to write fun slogans across the bag or create a sparkling design. ☆ Use some studs to create a pattern or use them to write a name. ☆ If you and a couple of friends have bags made of fabric, why not buy some beads and some special fabric glue between you, then spend a sleepover decorating them?

Fluffy Pens

Pens can look pretty dull, too, so why not cover them completely with some double-sided tape, stick some fun fur fabric over them from top to tip. You can do it with pencils too. It looks great!

Sparkle at School 59

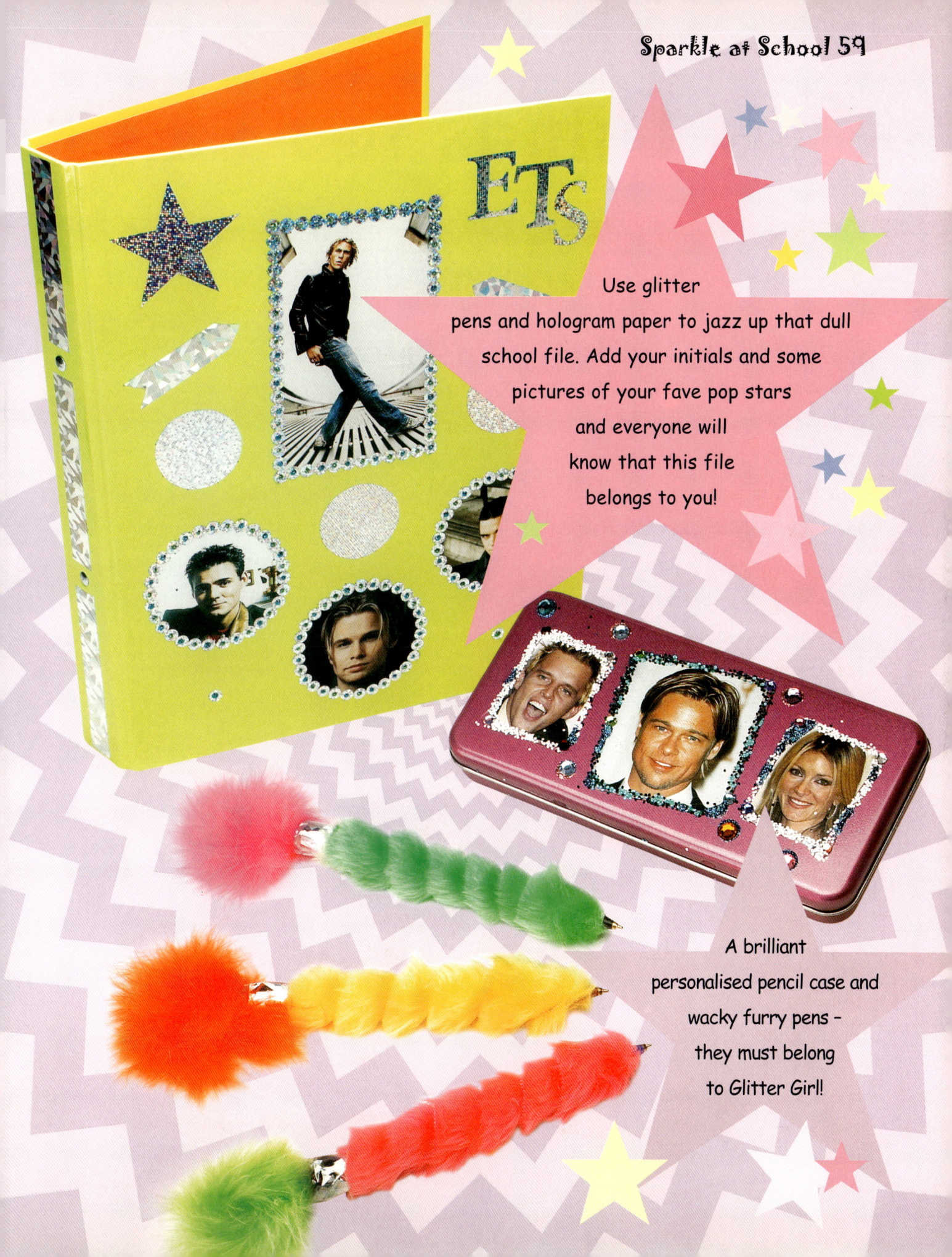

Use glitter pens and hologram paper to jazz up that dull school file. Add your initials and some pictures of your fave pop stars and everyone will know that this file belongs to you!

A brilliant personalised pencil case and wacky furry pens – they must belong to Glitter Girl!

/ Glitter Girl

Fab Things to Make

Feeling fun and creative, then why not make some special sparkly things for yourself or as gifts for your friends?

Desktop Pencil Holder

Turn one or several empty crisp tubes of different sizes into a super new desktop pencil holder. ☆ Paint the outsides and jazz them up with glitter, cut out stars and stick them all over, or cover them in holographic paper and tape. ☆ Glue tinsel around or use glitter pens to design your own creation or dip the rim into glue and then into fine glitter for a really great effect. ☆ Glue the tubes together and you've got a desk-top holder for all your school pens, pencils and rulers.

Trinket Box

A special trinket box is just what every girl needs to keep her favourite jewels in and this one is so simple to make.
☆ Cover a square tissue box with glittery wrapping paper.
☆ Use two different colours and add a line of glitter glue along the join.
☆ Glue on fake gems and you have a terrific trinket box.

Fab Things To Make 61

Glitter Room

If you would like to liven up your bedroom decor, give it the glitter treatment.

Mirror, Mirror...
Wake up to a glamorous glitter mirror.

YOU WILL NEED: cardboard • pen • scissors • sticky tape • mirror • spray glitter • gems

☆ Draw some shapes such as petals, flowers, raindrops, circles or moon shapes out on to a piece of cardboard.
☆ Carefully cut the shapes out to create the templates from which to work.
☆ Hold each template down firmly on the mirror with some sticky tape before spraying inside the shape with glitter or paint.
☆ Leave them for a few seconds to dry and then carefully remove the template.
☆ You'll be impressed with the results.

Other Ideas
☆ Put down lots of newspaper and spray a row of glitter carefully around the edge of the mirror.
☆ As a special gift for a friend, why not buy a mirror tile from your local DIY shop and personalize it with glitter or transfers?

A Touch of Luxury
☆ Cover plastic or wooden clothes hangers with wadding to make them soft and padded.
☆ Then cover with sparkly fabric, stitch in place and wind ribbon around the hook.
☆ Decorate with ribbon and beads or pompoms.
☆ They look really great and make welcome presents for friends and family too!

Glitter Room 63

For a great classic look, paint the mirror frame and stick some gems on to the mirror glass.

Fab Fingers

It's different, it's original and it's so easy to make - a jewellery tree to hang all your glistening gems and jewels on.

Jewellery Tree

It looks amazing and your friends will all be wondering how you made it.

YOU WILL NEED: Loads of newspaper • old washing-up glove • scissors • string • plaster of Paris (available from most DIY shops) • metal coat hanger • paints and paintbrush • varnish

☆ Put down lots of newspaper to keep the room clean. ☆ Take an old washing-up glove and make two holes opposite each other, near the wrist. ☆ Thread a length of string through the holes and tie a large knot at each end of the string to stop it from pulling through the holes. ☆ Mix the plaster of Paris as described on the packet. ☆ When it is of the correct consistency pour it into the glove. ☆ Gently press each finger to remove any air bubbles. ☆ Hold the glove steady whilst the plaster is setting and tie the string on to a metal coat hanger. ☆ Hang it somewhere warm to set for at least 24 hours, or longer if you can. ☆ After that time, carefully begin to peel the glove free. ☆ If the plaster still feels slightly damp, this means it hasn't set properly, so leave it for another 12 hours. ☆ Once set you should have a perfectly formed plaster cast of a hand – you may have to ask an adult to gently sand down the base of the wrist so it will stand up straight. ☆ When dry, give it several coats of paint before covering with a coat of varnish for staying power. ☆ Decorate it with flower motifs, painted glitter shapes or glitter gems. ☆ Add rings on the fingers and necklaces or bracelets draped around the wrist.